FUN FACTS ABOUT
Farm Animals

Written by
**Carol Benanti
& Ray H. Miller**

Illustrated by
Andrew Crabtree

The ERTL Company, Inc. would like to thank the following associations, companies, individuals, and photographers who helped make Fun Facts About Farm Animals possible:

Jan Gary at the American Ostrich Association; Corel Corporation;
Farm Safety 4 Just Kids; Bonnie Nance of Rural Images, Owensboro, Kentucky;
and Stan Harris of the U.S. Department of Agriculture

PHOTO CREDITS

AMERICAN OSTRICH ASSOCIATION
Page 23 photo of ostrich courtesy of the American Ostrich Association.

COREL PROFESSIONAL PHOTOS
Cover photo collage courtesy of Corel Corp.
Page 5 photo of cows courtesy of Corel Corp.
Page 7 photo of pig courtesy of Corel Corp.
Page 9 photo of chickens courtesy of Corel Corp.
Page 11 photo of sheep courtesy of Corel Corp.
Page 13 photo of cow courtesy of Corel Corp.
Page 17 photo of ducks courtesy of Corel Corp.
Page 19 photo of goat courtesy of Corel Corp.
Page 21 photo of horse and pony courtesy of Corel Corp.
Page 27 photo of turkey courtesy of Corel Corp.
Page 29 photo of llama courtesy of Corel Corp.

RURAL IMAGES
Page 25 photo of donkey courtesy of Bonnie Nance.

U.S. DEPARTMENT OF AGRICULTURE
Page 15 photo of dog courtesy of the U.S.D.A.

Printed in the U.S.A.
ISBN 1-887327-01-0
10 9 8 7 6 5 4 3 2 1

TABLE OF CONTENTS

DOWN ON THE FARM

Fun Facts About Farm Animals will show you a side of farm animals you've never seen. This book takes a look at some ordinary farm animals with some extraordinary habits and accomplishments. Whether they're cows, pigs, chickens, or llamas, you'll find out that there's more to our furry and feathered friends than just milk and eggs.

Why do some farmers play bluegrass music for their dairy cows? How could a sheep survive being buried for two months in a snowdrift? Which farm animal has ears as long as a baseball bat? Keep turning the pages of *Fun Facts About Farm Animals* to find out the answers to these questions, and much, much more.

PIGS

"Man is more nearly like a pig, than the pig wants to admit." This is just one famous quote about the lovable, intelligent pig. And you know what? It's true. People and pigs are similar. Other than raising pigs for food, the second most common commercial use of pigs is as medicine for people. A pig's heart has been used to replace a human heart. Read on to find out a few other things you probably didn't know about pigs.

SMART AS A PIG?

Most people think of pigs as dirty, lazy animals because they roll around in mud and dirt most of the day. Actually, pigs are one of the smartest and cleanest animals on the farm.

A pig doesn't have any sweat glands to help keep its body temperature low. Pigs know that rolling around in the cold, wet mud keeps their large bodies cool and very comfortable. For a pig, that sounds like a smart idea!

PIG OUT!

Americans eat more than 16 billion pounds of bacon, ham, and pork each year. If all this meat were made into hot dogs and laid end to end, it would reach from Earth to the moon more than 54 times.

A TON OF PIG

The largest pig on record is a Poland-China hog named Big Bull. Big Bull was raised in Tennessee in 1933. He was over 9 feet long and weighed 2,552 pounds. Big Bull weighed more than an average car!

HOG WILD

Can you imagine a pig like this one taking over an entire city? Of the 53 million hogs in the United States, 25% of them are in the state of Iowa. Imagine if all 53 million pigs were put together in one huge pen. That pen would take up almost the entire island of Manhattan, one of several boroughs of New York City. That's a small pen when compared to the one that would hold all 840 million pigs that live around the world. This gigantic pig pen would take up an area larger than the entire city of New York.

CHICKENS

"Don't Count Your Chickens Before They Hatch." In the chicken business, counting is important, and chicken farmers have to count their chickens, hatched or not. The largest chicken farm in the world is the Agrigeneral Company in Ohio. This giant farm has enough hens to lay 4 million eggs a day. In one year, all the eggs would cover nearly 1.5 square miles! Read on to see how chickens and their farmers have broken many other records.

SCRAMBLED OR OVER-EASY?

Can you imagine an entire family splitting one egg for breakfast? That could have happened on February 25, 1956. On that day in Vineland, New Jersey, a white leghorn chicken laid an extra-extra-large egg that weighed 1 full pound. This huge egg had not one, but two yolks, and was the size of eight "large" eggs.

SOAR LIKE A... CHICKEN?

Everyone knows chickens can't fly very far.

Everyone except "Flying Sheena," a barn-yard bantam chicken owned by Bill and

Bob Knox of Parkesburg, Pennsylvania. This crazy bird flew the farthest distance ever flown by a chicken. She soared over 630 feet on May 31, 1985. That's longer than the length of two football fields.

NOW THAT'S A CLUCKER PLUCKER!

Many have tried to perfect the art of chicken-plucking. But no one did it better than Ernest Hausen of Fort Atkinson, Wisconsin.

On January 19, 1939, Ernest plucked a chicken clean in 4.4 seconds. If Ernest had kept plucking at that rate, he would have plucked over 800 chickens in one hour.

GO LAY AN EGG

These white Leghorn chickens lay an average of 245 eggs each year. Another white Leghorn chicken, named "No. 2988" didn't think that was good enough. This commercial chicken laid the most chicken eggs ever – 371 eggs in 364 days. This incredible, record-breaking event took place at the College of Agriculture, University of Missouri, on August 29, 1979. If all the eggs "No. 2988" laid in one year were laid end to end, they would stretch from one end of a professional basketball court to the other.

SHEEP

Sheep are a favorite farm animal for many reasons. Besides being fun to play with when they're frisky lambs, farmers value sheep for their fleecy hair. The hair from one sheep produces almost 2 pounds of clean, soft wool. All the sheep in the United States would produce enough wool to make almost 18 million sweaters – one for every person in the state of New York. Here are some other amazing facts about sheep that will surprise you.

THE KING OF SHEEP

Have you ever seen a sheep as big as a lion? Joseph and Susan Schallberger of Boring, Oregon, own a sheep named "Stratford Whisper 23H." In 1991, this giant Suffolk ram weighed in at 545 pounds and stood 43 inches tall. An average ram weighs about 300 pounds, so "Stratford" is definitely king of the sheep.

INSTANT HERD

Most female sheep, called *ewes*, have one or two baby lambs at a time. But a four-year-old Suffolk ewe owned by Gerry H. Watson of Augusta, Kansas, was in a hurry for a big family. On January 30, 1982, she gave birth to *two sets of healthy triplets*. The six lambs together weighed almost 50 pounds.

DANCING SHEEP TO SHEEP

There are over 10 million sheep in the United States. Texas leads the country with two million sheep. If all the sheep in the U.S. started a line dance at a county fair in New York, that wild 'n' wooly line would stretch across America to San Francisco almost four times.

SNOW SHEEP

This little lamb probably doesn't have to "count sheep" before falling asleep. It often leads a quiet life on the farm spending time with its mother and roaming the fields. Not all sheep are this lucky. On March 24, 1978, a man named Alex Maclennan dug out a healthy female sheep from a snowdrift. She had been there since a January blizzard. Her breath made air holes in the snow for her to breathe. To stay alive, she gnawed on her wool for protein. And of course, she had her own natural wool "sweater" to keep her warm.

COWS

American cows prefer bluegrass! Bluegrass music, that is. Some farmers have found that playing bluegrass music while milking their cows seems to calm the animals – and results in more milk! One cow named "No. 289" produced the most milk of any cow in history – over 54,000 gallons. That's almost enough milk to fill three average-sized in-ground swimming pools. Do you suppose "No. 289" was listening to bluegrass music?

MARATHON MILKING

Expert "hand-milkers" could milk 12 cows in one hour. Can you imagine milking cows for 12 hours nonstop? A man named Andy Faust from Collinsville, Oklahoma, holds the American record for hand-milking. Andy milked over 88 gallons of milk in 12 hours. That's over 7 gallons an hour!

AN EATING MACHINE

Would you believe that cows have four stomachs? Actually, they have only one true stomach, but it has four compartments. Cows chew their food only enough to swallow it. Once it reaches the first two stomachs, it is turned into softened food called *cud*. The cud is then sent back up to the cow's mouth, where it is chewed and swallowed again. Finally, the cud is sent to the last two stomachs where it is digested. Do you suppose when a cow gets a stomach ache, it hurts four times as much?

A LOT OF BULL

The heaviest bull on record, named "Mount Katahdin," was exhibited in Maine from 1906 to 1910. He stood 6 feet 2 inches tall at the shoulder and weighed 5,000 pounds. That's the same weight as two average-sized hippopotamuses.

LAWN MOO-ERS

You may never need to mow the lawn again if you keep a cow around. An average 1,500 pound dairy cow – like this Holstein-Friesian – will eat 15 pounds of hay, and 45 pounds of *silage*, or chopped corn stalks, each day in the winter. Farmers also feed them a pound of grain for every 3 gallons of milk they produce. During the summer, when cows graze in the fields, they keep the pasture perfectly manicured. In one year, a dairy cow will eat over 10 tons of grass, hay and grain. That's over 15 times the cow's weight in food.

DOGS & CATS

"It's raining cats and dogs." There are over 52 million dogs and 63 million cats in the U.S. Some of these dogs and cats live on farms. Cats keep barns mice-free, and farm dogs protect cattle and sheep. Dogs that live on big ranches help move large herds from the field to the barn. Herding dogs learn to respond to hand signals from the ranchers, and move the herd by nipping at their heels. Let's take a look at some extraordinary dogs and cats.

FULL-COURT KITTIES

A tabby cat named "Dusty," born in 1935 in Bonham, Texas, produced 420 kittens in her lifetime, the most of any cat on record. If all of Dusty's offspring had to wait in line for a kitty treat, that line would be longer than three basketball courts, and Dusty's kittens could have formed 84 teams to play while they waited.

RICH POOCH

The wealthiest dog ever was a poodle named "Toby." Toby's owner, Ella Wendel of New York left Toby $75 million when she died in 1931. Today, Toby's inheritance could buy 10 yachts, 10 Learjets, a different limousine for every day of the year, 10 solid gold collars, each with 25 one-carat diamonds, and 180,000 pounds of prime steak.

MORE TO LOVE

The heaviest and longest dog ever recorded is an Old English mastiff named "Zorba." In November 1989, Zorba was living in London, Great Britain, with his owner, Chris Eraclides.

At that time, Zorba was 8 feet 3 inches long and weighed 343 pounds, which is as big as a full-grown tiger.

HAVE YOU "HERD?"

Farmers will often have a retriever, collie, or sheepdog to help herd and protect the animals. When they aren't busy herding, these dogs sometimes lay among the animals in the field and keep a watchful eye on them as they graze, like this faithful retriever is doing. An Australian cattle-dog named "Bluey" happens to be the oldest dog ever. Bluey was owned by Les Hall of Victoria, Australia. Les adopted Bluey as a puppy in 1910, and they were still together 29 years later. Bluey worked hard at herding and protecting cattle and sheep for almost 20 years.

DUCKS & GEESE

Ducks and geese are members of the same family, but these cousins are very different. Geese are "landlubbers" and eat grass and weeds. In fact, baby geese, called *goslings*, are natural weed-eaters. Ducks, however, are water lovers. Their undersides are flat and perfect for floating, and their webbed feet are great for paddling. Ducks can dip their heads underwater to find food. Now we'll let you in on some secrets about our feathered friends.

DON'T HOLD YOUR BREATH

Ducks are experts at diving to the bottom of ponds and lakes. They can go for long periods of time without coming up for air.

In fact, ducks can swim underwater for distances of 300 feet, which is almost the length of four tennis courts.

EGG-CEPTIONAL

Goose eggs are very large. A large chicken egg weighs 2 ounces, but a goose egg weighs between 10 and 12 ounces. The biggest

goose egg ever recorded came from a white goose named "Speckle," owned by Donny Brandenberg of Goshen, Ohio. On May 3, 1977, Speckle laid an egg that weighed 24 ounces and measured more than 13 inches long and 9 inches wide. That's bigger than a professional football.

GREAT GANDER GOOSE!

Most geese on farms live to about 25 years old.

George, a gander (male) goose, born in 1927, lived almost twice as long. He lived until he was 49 years old! That's a record for domestic birds.

DABBLING DUCK

Imagine you're in a concert hall waiting for a pianist to walk on stage. He finally appears, only he's waddling, not walking. He approaches a tiny piano, flips his white tails, and plays a perfect classic melody. No, you're not dreaming. You're watching Burt, an amazing musical duck that has been trained by Animal Behavior Enterprises (ABE). The ABE trains animals to do more than entertain – some have been involved in top secret government projects. Wonder if any of these geese will ever get trained to read?

GOATS

Where can you go to get a sweater, leather boots, cheese, fudge, and soap? You could go to many different stores, or simply raise goats. A type of goat's wool, called *mohair*, is used to make fabric for drapes and furniture, and *cashmere* from goat's wool is used to make soft clothing. A goat's hide makes wonderful leather, and goat's milk is used to make soaps, fudge, and cheeses. Keep reading for other reasons goats are farm favorites.

UDDERLY AMAZING

Most female goats give milk only for about ten months. But Carolyn Freund-Nelson of Northport, New York, has had to milk her goat, nicknamed "Baba," every day for the past 13 years. If all of Baba's milk was poured into eight-ounce glasses and stacked on top of each other, that tower of glasses would reach from the ground floor to the top of the Empire State Building 15 times.

MILES OF MOHAIR

Farmers raise Angora goats because their long, six-inch wool can be made into mohair. There are about 1.3 million Angora

goats in the United States. If you took 20 strands of wool from each Angora goat and tied them together, that combined string of wool would stretch over 2,000 miles, which is almost as long as the Mississippi River.

NOW THAT'S ITALIAN!

There are 3 million goats in the U.S., and each goat produces an average of 2 quarts of milk a day. All the goat milk produced in one year could make enough ricotta cheese to feed every person in the state of Arkansas one bowl of ravioli.

SMOKY THE GOAT

Some goats will do just about anything for a mouthful of leaves, grass, and plants – they'll even climb down steep steps for an afternoon snack. The United States Forest Service (USFS) decided to take advantage of the goat's eagerness to eat. The USFS uses as many as 800 goats to keep the Cleveland National Forest in Southern California clear of brush and leaves. During hot weather, these leaves and brush can cause dangerous fires. Thanks to a lot of hungry goats, this area stays brush-free.

HORSES

At one time, horses were used to pull wagons and plows on the farm. Now that machines do most of the work, horses are raised mostly for riding and racing. Thoroughbred race-horses can run a mile in about a minute and a half. A person traveling across the entire state of Indiana on foot would take close to two days. A thoroughbred horse could run across Indiana in less than four hours. Let's look at some really special horses.

MICRO HORSE
Can you imagine carrying a horse across the street? That would have been easy for J. C. Williams Jr. of Inman, South Carolina. In 1975, he raised a miniature stallion, named "Little Pumpkin" on his farm, the Della Terra Mini Horse Farm. Full grown, Little Pumpkin stood only 14 inches high and weighed just 20 pounds.

DOOR-TO-DOOR HORSE
The tallest and heaviest horse ever recorded lived in 1850 and was

named "Mammoth." He stood 7 feet 2½ inches tall and weighed over 3,000 pounds. Mammoth probably wouldn't have been a very good door-to-door sales-man since the average door on a house is only 7 feet high.

HORSE POWER
Big work horses, like the Belgian and the Clydes-dale, once provided the power needed to do the work that tractors do today. They were so strong that each horse could pull a load weighing more than 2,000 pounds. One of those work horses could easily pull a wagonload of 8 baby African elephants.

HORSE SENSE

Can you tell what these two horses are thinking? A special mind-reading horse named "Lady," from Richmond, Virginia, probably could. For almost 30 years Lady "spoke" to people by writing letters with her muzzle on a board. She supposedly predicted Harry Truman's presidential victory in 1948, and she helped police find a missing child by writing down the child's location. Psychologists tried to prove that Lady wrote down whatever her owner signaled her to write. They never found any evidence of foul play, however.

OSTRICHES

Most people picture ostriches running across the deserts of Africa. But did you know there are 100,000 ostriches in the United States? They are raised mostly for their meat, which according to Glenda Camp of the Grand Oaks Ostrich Ranch in Vernon, Florida, tastes just like beef. Glenda challenges anyone to tell the difference between her ostrich burger and a hamburger. Read on to find out other things about ostriches that will surprise you.

AEROBIC OSTRICH

Ostriches are the largest birds in the world and can grow to be 9 feet tall and weigh 345 pounds.

Even though the ostrich is a big, strong bird, it can't fly. But the ostrich is the fastest bird on land. It takes giant 15-foot steps and can run 40 miles an hour for up to 30 minutes.

If it didn't have to stop for traffic lights, an ostrich could run the length of the island of Manhattan in New York City in less than 15 minutes.

SUPER VISION

Ostrich eyes are very large and these big birds have keen eyesight. An ostrich can see objects up to 7 miles away. If you could see that far, you would be able to read the name on a jet flying in the sky overhead.

BRUNCH, ANYONE?

Ostrich eggs weigh up to 3 pounds! The next time you want a soft-boiled egg for breakfast, make sure the cook isn't serving ostrich eggs. Ostrich eggs are so big that it would take 40 minutes to boil just one.

NO ORDINARY BIRD

Ostriches are a big help to mankind in many ways. The strong tendons in their long, powerful legs are used for tendon transplants in people. Ostrich eyes are used for research in optometry schools, and their corneas are being trimmed down in size for cornea transplants in humans. Medical researchers have even discovered that the brain of an ostrich produces a certain enzyme that is now being used to study Alzheimer's Disease. We owe a lot to this giant bird.

DONKEYS

Learning all the members of the donkey family can prove to be a bit confusing. A female donkey is called a *jenny*, and a male is called a *jack*. If a jack is crossed with a female horse, or *mare*, the animal that is born is called a *mule*. If a jenny is crossed with a male horse, or *stallion*, the animal that is born is called a *hinny*. Small donkeys are called *burros*. Now that we've got that straight, let's find out more about donkeys and mules.

SEVENTH-INNING STRETCH

The largest breed of donkey in the world is called the American Mammoth jackstock. It stands almost 5 feet high at the shoulder, and weighs more than five grown men. The most unique thing about the jackstock is its long jackrabbit-like ears. If you stretched a jackstock's ears out flat, and measured them from end to end, they would be about as long as a major league baseball bat.

DONKEY SURPRISE

Mules have always been considered to be unable to reproduce. But in Nebraska in 1984, the impossible happened. A

mule named "Krause" and a donkey named "Chester" produced a baby donkey, or *foal*, named "Blue Moon." A U.S. Congressman was so excited by this news that he proposed October 28 be known as Mule Appreciation Day.

DONKEY DEAL

Looking for a bargain?

At a sale in South Africa in 1934, donkeys were sold for less than 5 cents each – the lowest price ever paid for livestock. For less than what it costs to buy a pack of gum today, they got a whole pack of donkeys!

SOLITARY DONKEY

Mother and baby donkeys love to spend time together, whether it's while eating or resting in the field. But did you know a donkey named "Islander" spent 18 years of his life alone? When an island near Ireland was evacuated in 1967, somebody forgot to take poor Islander. He had plenty of grass and seaweed to eat, and an occasional visiting fisherman would trim his hooves. But life for Islander must have been pretty lonely. Finally, Islander was rescued and taken to an animal sanctuary where he had plenty of company.

TURKEYS

Native Americans once raised turkeys for much more than just food. In the past, they used turkey bones to make spoons and beads. Turkey claws were made into arrowheads. And turkey feathers were used to make warm cloaks for winter. Because it is native to North America, Benjamin Franklin wanted the turkey, instead of the bald eagle, to be our national bird. Here are a few other things about this truly American bird you probably didn't know.

GOBBLE, GOBBLE

Do you think you could eat 60 turkey sandwiches?

That's how much turkey each person in the United States eats every year.

TONS O' TURKEY

North Carolina raises 58 million turkeys each year. That comes to 580,000 tons of meat.

If all the turkeys in North Carolina got their passports and went to visit the Queen of England, it would take nearly seven aircraft carriers to carry them across the Atlantic Ocean.

DRUMSTICK, ANYONE?

Would you ever pay 87 dollars a pound for a turkey dinner?

The biggest turkey ever stuffed and served on a platter weighed 86 pounds. It was raised by Philip Cook of Leacroft Turkeys in Great Britain. On December 12, 1989, it won the "heaviest turkey" competition in London and was auctioned for charity for a record price of $7,480.

BIRDS OF A FEATHER?

Wild turkeys are very different from the domestic turkeys we eat. Wild turkeys are powerful, intelligent birds with shiny multi-colored feathers. If threatened, they can spread their 5- to 6-foot wings and fly at speeds up to 50 miles an hour. Most domestic turkeys have white feathers and can't fly at all because they are too heavy, so it would be very difficult for them to survive in the wild. They are friendlier and will approach people, but they'll let out a loud "gobble" if you surprise them.

LLAMAS

Originally from South America, llamas can be found in every state in the U.S. Smaller than its cousin, the camel, a llama stands up to 5 feet tall at the shoulders. Llamas are perfect for taking on hikes, camping trips, and when studying remote forests and wilderness. Llamas are very smart, and farmers raise them as pets, as guards for their sheep, and for their long, thick wool. Keep reading to find out other fascinating facts about llamas.

LLAMA-RAMA
Santa Claus and his 8 tiny reindeer are no match for Floyd Zopfi of Stratford, Wisconsin. Floyd has driven as many as 52 llamas at once.

But if a llama feels it is carrying too much, or thinks it has walked far enough, it will simply stop, lie down, and take a break.

The llamas are harnessed in four rows, and the leading llamas are on reins that are 150 feet long. That's a line of llamas as long as half a city block.

GET OFF MY BACK
Because llamas are sure-footed and easy-going, they are used as "pack" animals. A llama could easily carry a child across Honolulu, Hawaii, in one day.

THE LLAMA BOWL
There are 70,000 llamas in the United States.

If all the llamas in the U.S. went to a football game, they would fill every seat in the Louisiana Super Dome.

SAFETY TIPS

A farm is a wonderful place to live and visit. Animals are an important part of many farm operations and can be a lot of fun. But life on a farm can sometimes be dangerous. Animals can get startled, which can lead to dangerous situations. Here are some smart safety tips to keep in mind while around farm animals:

1. Be calm and quiet around farm animals. Always approach animals with caution.

2. Farm animals can be unpredictable. Don't ever stand behind large animals, such as bulls, cows, rams, or horses. They could become threatened and kick you. Stay behind a fence if you want to see the animals.

3. Don't ever approach baby animals, because mothers are very protective. Mother animals can cause severe injuries if they think you are trying to harm their young.

4. Even smaller farm animals are full of surprises. An angry rooster can deliver a painful kick with its spurs – the sharp claws on the backs of its legs. Always have adult supervision when working around farm animals.

Because farm life involves being outdoors and around many animals, sometimes a farm can seem like a large playground. But living and working on a farm has many hazards. Farm Safety 4 Just Kids works to prevent farm-related childhood injuries, health risks, and fatalities. Contact the organization at 1-800-423-KIDS to learn more about staying safe on the farm. A healthy and safe farm is a happy farm, so always stay alert.

Order The Replica

Whether you are a serious collector or just a big fan of farm toys, you should consider a subscription to <u>The Replica</u>. This 4-color, bi-monthly magazine comes to you direct from The Ertl Company. It's full of the latest news about upcoming product releases in die cast farm toys, farm playsets, banks and other Ertl collectibles. And, from time to time, special subscriber-only, exclusive products are offered.

To receive your subscription of <u>The Replica</u>, write to:

The Ertl Company Replica Offer
Dept. 776A Highways 136 & 20
P.O. Box 500, Dyersville, IA 52040-0500

Inside the U.S.A. $10.00 for 1 year and $18.00 for 2 years
Outside the U.S.A. $14.00 for 1 year and $22.00 for 2 years

Farm Safety ♥ Just Kids

For more information on how to stay safe on the farm, call or write:

Farm Safety 4 Just Kids
110 South Chestnut Avenue
P.O. Box 458
Earlham, IA 50072

1-800-423-KIDS or 1-515-758-2827

Fun Facts About Farm Animals was created in cooperation with Farm Safety 4 Just Kids.